NAKED TRUTHS
About Getting Book Reviews
2018

Copyright © 2018 by Gisela Hausmann
Published by Educ-Easy Books via CreateSpace

* * *

Earlier editions:

NAKED TRUTHS About Getting Book Reviews **(2015)**

NAKED TRUTHS About Getting Book Reviews
Fully Revised and Updated **(2016)**

NAKED REVIEW
How to Get Book Reviews
What to do now that Amazon closed all loopholes **(2017)**

* * *

Editor:
Divya Lavanya M.

* * *

CONTENT

Prerequisite   8

All books need more reviews   9

That's Me   11

Unqualified advice   13

Understanding Amazon's Review Platform   17

10 Different Kinds of Reviews   21

The Starter Review   23

The "Verified" Friend's, Fan's, and Follower's Review   30

The Review Club Review   33

The Goodreads Review   38

Regular Customer Reviews   42

Book Signing Event Attendees' reviews   43

Real Life Author Group Member's reviews   45

The Top Reviewer's or Hall of Fame Reviewer's Review   48

Negative Reviews   50

Troll Reviews   52

Getting to work   55

Always remember – Your book needs diversity of opinions!   57

Authors' communication skills   59

"Looks good" vs. "This is what I have been looking for"   65

More About Building a Fan Base   67

Spread enthusiasm, passionately!   72

7 Thoughts to Keep You Going   75

Other books by Gisela Hausmann   87

About the Author   91

Prerequisite

Here's a link to Amazon's community guidelines for posting reviews.

http://www.amazon.com/gp/community-help/customer-reviews-guidelines

It is immensely important that you study these review guidelines and re-read them every month! Nobody knows when Amazon decides to make changes. During the last two years, Amazon changed its community guidelines four times without warning.

Always re-read the guidelines before you launch a promotion that is geared at receiving many book reviews.

All Books Need More reviews

- "My book needs more reviews!"

- "Even after I ran a free promo, less than 1% of people who downloaded it also reviewed it."

- "I want better/longer/more exciting reviews."

Comments like these can be found in authors' discussion groups on many social media platforms. Less frustrated-sounding social media postings ask to "Save an Author", "Support an Author", and "Hug an Author" by reading and reviewing independent authors' books.

Every day, on average, thirty-one authors tweet "(Please) post a Review." Typically, the tweets reach around 140+K Twitter accounts. The fight is real. It is hard to get book reviews and even harder to get great book reviews. The fact that every month more people publish more books does not help.

Reviews follow the "law of attraction"

Though this may sound unfair, the truth is that the more reviews a book receives, the more people will add their own opinions, even though their thoughts may have already been expressed in previous reviews.

To date, "Fifty Shades of Grey (Fifty Shades, Book 1)" by E L James, which was released May 25, 2011, received 84,957 customer reviews.

Even more surprisingly, the book received four reviews on Christmas Eve, 2017 and 74 reviews between December 1 and December 25, 2017, six years after the book made waves upon its release.

I know what you are thinking.

"I am not jealous, but, objectively, E L James' book doesn't need any more reviews. It already has 84K+ reviews."

And,

"Why is it so hard for me to get people to review my book?"

It's all about the "law of attraction." Whether you believe in it or not, for sure it applies to getting book reviews.

Even though people who review E L James' book have to assume that one of the more than 84,000 reviewers came to the very same conclusion as they did, they will still add their opinions.

The same is true for products. Amazon's Fire TV Stick with Alexa Voice Remote | Streaming Media Player received 126,050 reviews.

Hence, the question is, how do you get the process going? To clarify this matter is the subject of this book.

That's Me

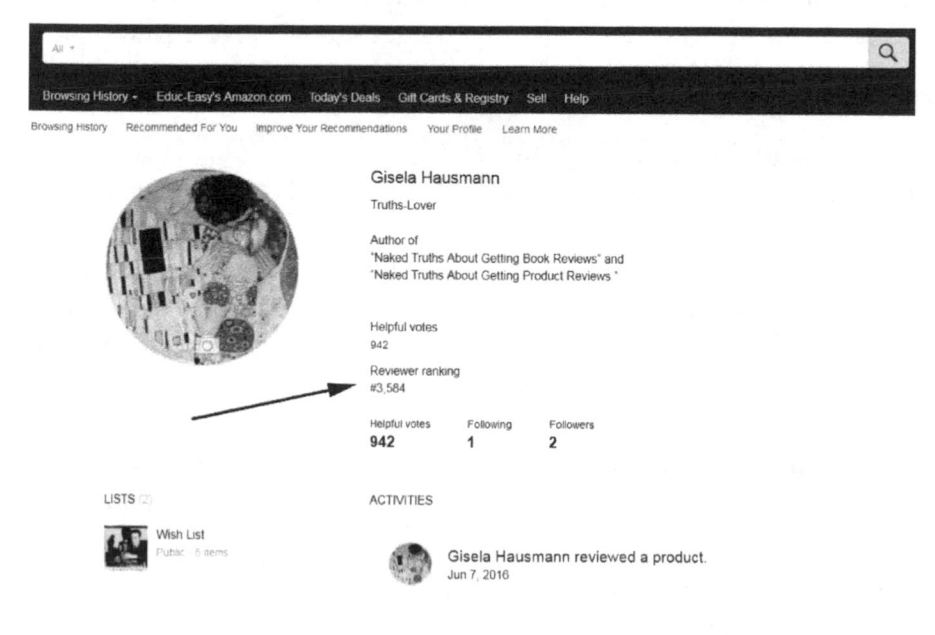

Gisela Hausmann
Truths-Lover

Author of
"Naked Truths About Getting Book Reviews" and
"Naked Truths About Getting Product Reviews "

Helpful votes
942

Reviewer ranking
#3,584

Helpful votes	Following	Followers
942	1	2

LISTS (2)

Wish List
Public 5 items

ACTIVITIES

Gisela Hausmann reviewed a product.
Jun 7, 2016

Hello, I am Gisela Hausmann. I have written and published twenty-five books since 1988. I began reviewing at Amazon in 2012. In 2014, I reached Amazon Top Reviewer ranking, consistently being ranked among Amazon's Top-10,000 of more than fifty million reviewers. My best ranking was #2,756.

I reached this excellent ranking by reviewing Hillary Clinton's memoir "What Happened." Though, eventually I had to delete this review after I got trolled extensively by both HRC's friends and enemies, this example explains one problem Amazon top reviewers and indie authors face together (It's not about trolls).

The issue is – reviewing a book that received a lot of attention results in the review getting noticed and getting "liked" more often.

Naturally, you might say, "Well, isn't that to be expected?" Of course it is, but there is also the problem – these days many authors who get in the industry unprepared give up.

Obviously, whenever this happens a reviewer must ask themselves if they picked the wrong book. Since the author won't market their book anymore, the review won't be seen any longer. Maybe the reviewer should have picked another author's book?

This recognition prompts me and probably a lot of other top reviewers to take a very close look at books and their authors.

Therefore, my first advice to you is: Whatever you do, always show that you are in for the long haul when communicating with influencers. Minimal effort won't get you anywhere because the market is flooded with good books.

no "one & done."

To be precise, you *always* need to demonstrate that you are serious about this business.

Even your friends want your assurance that they aren't wasting their time. They too want to believe that they are reading your book because you are working hard on becoming the next J.K. Rowling or Stephen King. If you can convey this notion, they'll be more inclined to (a) read your book and (b) spread the word.

Nobody wants to be a person who wasted their precious leisure time and everybody wants to be that "well connected" person who read the next bestselling author's book first.

Once you embark on the journey to becoming an author, you represent your brand and you are your brand's spokesperson. Hence, show your dedication. Nobody is going to do it for you!

*

Maybe you think that this is banal advice. It's not.
Only last month, I received a message from an author friend who asked me, "Hey Gisela, would you like to read my next book? I have decided that I am going to give Sci-Fi a try."

Keeping aside the fact that the author directed his/her question at the wrong person (it's well known that I don't read Sci-Fi), the question is a lame question.

The explanation, "I want to give this or that genre a try" does not radiate any motivation, commitment, or excitement, which are precisely the qualities that convince people to pick a book.

In short: To succeed, you need to be your own cheerleader and also your readers' cheerleader!

There are hundreds of ways you can do this.

For instance, if you and a friend who read your book meet with other friends, why not mention casually, "Yep, Charlie was the first person to read my latest novel." I can guarantee you that your other friends will be more interested in reading "the book Charlie already read" than "a book of a genre you wanted to give a try."

This is the world we live in.

The first rule of indie author book marketing is: To get reviews – Be your readers' cheerleader!

Unqualified advice

Still, the biggest problem for authors who seek book reviews is the fact that seemingly everybody and their grandmother publishes a book. This results in the following problems:

- The book market is flooded with good and also not-so-good books; more and more authors have to share the same number of readers.
- In order to gain attention, too many authors offer their books for free; on any given day, Amazon carries more than 60,000 free books.
- As a result, tens of thousands of readers hoard free books they may never read, which means authors do not get any return (reviews and/or word of mouth promotion) for their free-give-away promos.
- To make matters worse, some members of reviews clubs award each other with "inflated" 5-star reviews. Lately, the number of book reviews that state "I don't know why this book has so many 5-star reviews; are all these readers friends of the author..." is on the rise again.
- Lastly, maybe, the biggest problem of all is that too many newbie authors don't learn how the industry works from the ground up. Consequently, they make mistakes that affect all authors.

This last bullet point may require an explanation:
For instance, one of these errors was that thousands of indie authors followed some bloggers' advice to "attach .mobi files of their books when contacting Amazon top reviewers."

It's _not_ a clever advice!
Using electronic messaging systems to send unsolicited materials is called SPAM, hence it isn't appreciated, especially by reviewers who receive many requests.

Newbie authors probably can't even imagine what it was like for me receiving between five and ten unsolicited ebooks per week. It's is like people inviting themselves to stay at your house or storing stuff in your garage. In November 2016, I finally had enough and removed my email address from Amazon's site. This happened even though I was never ranked in the top-1,000.

When I surveyed quite many Hall-of-Fame reviewers in Spring 2016, most of them received an average of 230+ review requests per week, hence they may have received fifty to sixty unsolicited ebooks per week.

The efforts of thousands of authors who followed this silly and totally improper suggestion from unqualified author-bloggers resulted in many of Amazon's top reviewers deleting their email addresses and some of them even making their profiles "invisible."

To see what "invisible profiles" look like, please go to https://www.amazon.com/review/top-reviewers and click on the top reviewers' names.

Even though some of these most active reviewers review between 40 and 50 items per week, their profiles don't show what kind of books and products they read and review.

Eventually, in March 2017, Amazon disconnected all top reviewers' email addresses. Though I have no idea why they did it, I can envision that upon hearing about this rampant abuse, one of Amazon's corporate lawyers advised that the company might be accused of enabling SPAM if they allowed spammers to contact their top reviewers via their website.

In short, the reason why the glorious days of 2008 to 2016 when about 5,000 of Amazon's 10,000 top reviewers reviewed indie author books came to an end was that huge numbers of indie authors followed bad advice from unqualified author bloggers who call themselves "experts," but really aren't.

So, what can blog readers do to avoid acting upon incorrect information?

1) Remember the First Amendment
When reading a blog, always remember that in the United States the First Amendment guarantees people the right to write even about things they know nothing about or can't prove to be true. Therefore:

2) Check the blogger's background!
Every blogger features a short resume at the beginning or the end of their blog. Always study it; if need be – verify it. Don't hesitate to ask poignant questions.
As I just explained, an author-blogger who does not actually review themselves does not know the thinking of a reviewer because, obviously, only people who actually "do the task" have insider information.

3) Check the date!
If a blog is older than six months, chances are at least some parts may be outdated. Things change quickly these days.

Understanding Amazon's Review Platform

To truly understand how Amazon's review platform works, we need to first accept that, just like Google and Facebook, Amazon is a huge data collector.

Put in the most simple terms, this means small efforts, like calling your five best friends and asking them to read and review your book probably won't have any affect at all. Most likely, Amazon assumes anyway that you'll be trying this avenue. It's only normal that authors want their friends to read their books.

On the other hand, if authors follow unprofessional advice like the already mentioned, "attach a .mobi file to your review request," which equates to spamming top reviewers, the actions can have huge implications.

An easy way to figure out whether a planned action might cause issues is to ponder what will happen if 1,000 authors follow the exact same advice.

In the first scenario, 1,000 authors may each gain five reviews from friends/people who probably won't criticize their work in public.

Not a big deal! Considering that Amazon's review platform hosts more than a billion reviews, Amazon probably won't even notice.

In the second scenario, individual Hall-of-Fame reviewers will receive up to 1,000 review requests with ebooks attached. Certainly, this effort will be noticed, but not in a good way.

*

Though, in Facebook author groups, many authors speculate that Amazon does not support indie authors' marketing efforts and deletes their reviews purposely, this is not true. For starters, there is no person at Amazon who deletes reviews; Amazon's famous algorithm does the "dirty work." However, with the help of AI (artificial intelligence), human programmers configure Amazon's algorithm based on trends.

Certainly, Amazon adjusts its algorithm to counter the cheating efforts of authors and product vendors. In fact, Amazon doesn't really have a choice. Since Amazon is a global ecommerce platform, they have to support the FTC's (Federal Trade Commission) truth-in-advertising laws. This equates to hindering people from posting fake reviews. To learn more about this topic, please go to

https://www.ftc.gov/tips-advice/business-center/advertising-and-marketing/online-advertising-and-marketing
and
http://www.amazon.com/gp/community-help/customer-reviews-guidelines

Therefore, when authors cheat, they literally force Amazon to adjust their algorithms.

Every time an author comes up with a *creative method* to bypass best practices in review seeking and *reveals their method* in a blog, this causes a snowball effect, which culminates in Amazon tightening their algorithms.

The worst thing about this situation is that it not only affects the cheating authors but also the innocent authors who get caught in the crossfire. Often, I hear authors complaining that some of their reviews got deleted even though they don't do review exchanges. The reason is obvious – no algorithm can be perfect.

Additionally, not only authors *get caught in the crossfire* but reviewers too. That's because the more items a reviewer reviews, the more often their name pops up in algorithms' data searches.

Over the last one-and-a-half year, Amazon revoked the reviewer privileges of hundreds of top reviewers and even of Hall-of-Fame reviewers.

When a reviewer's review privileges get revoked, *all* reviews of all books and products he/she reviewed get deleted, at once. The reviewer loses years of work. Hence, for the last six to eight months, reviewers have been on high alert. I too avoid reviewing books from authors who might engage in any kind of activities I don't want to be associated with.

For instance, if I notice a book review that starts with the words "This book is..." I immediately check out other reviews from the same reviewer. If the reviewer begins more than one book review with the words "This book is..." I will not review any of the books this reviewer reviewed. Maybe the reviewer is part of a review club and "working off a list."

This is just one way how reviewers can spot review clubs' activities. Another one is to watch Amazon's suggestions of books listed in the section "Customers who viewed this item also viewed...". If the same books pop up all the time, obviously the author-reviewers are connected somehow.

It is important to understand that reviewers do not react this way because they are mean-spirited but because nobody likes to lose years of work. It's like going to college and dropping out before graduation.

Over the last few years, Amazon even "kicked out" 16 of 148 Hall-of-Fame reviewers; that's more than ten percent. The names and reviews of regular top reviewers whose reviewer privileges got revoked simply disappear (with all reviews), completely.

To see the damage in Hall-of-Fame reviewer circles, please go to
https://www.amazon.com/hz/leaderboard/hall-of-fame

Reviewers who have zero reviews to their name had their reviewer privileges revoked.

These and other problems ask for the question, "How do I get reviews – the proper way?"

Before we examine this question, let's first look at the different types of reviews.

10 Different Kinds of Reviews

It is important to understand that to attract buyers/readers, your book(s) should receive as many different types of reviews as possible, including negative reviews and possibly even one or two troll reviews.

Today, more than ever people seek confirmation of their beliefs. In this world of polarized opinions, people want to know that somebody sees things the way they see them. Hence, the more various kinds of reviews your book receives, the higher the chance that people will find the review (good or bad) they wanted to read.

Let's take the example of a book about any democratic president or presidential candidate:

- 5-star reviews probably confirm what loyal Democrats believe whereas they won't convince staunch Republicans that the book is a great book.

- 1-star reviews might convince even staunch Republicans to buy and read the book to find confirmation of their beliefs and also to have an opportunity to publicly vent about their opinions by reviewing the book.

In short, all reviews will help in selling a book, provided that they are emotional reviews which share personal feelings.

Please highlight this sentence: All reviews, good or bad, will help in selling a book, provided that they are **emotional reviews that share personal feelings and insights**. Of course, this statement excludes books that have mostly negative reviews.

Consumers don't necessarily want to read a retelling of your book's plot; in actuality, they want to know,

"How will I feel when I read this book?"

Will I

- find the information I am looking for
- feel smarter and more educated
- be provided with clever shortcuts or essential knowledge
- be dazzled with beautiful descriptions of events
- be taken to magical worlds
- be horrified by terrifying villains or fictitious end-of-the-world scenarios
- be charmed
- feel sexy

and, also

- Will I buy a book that teaches my child something I want her to know?

Today's indie authors can influence getting these kinds of reviews by carefully selecting people who will write great starter reviews.

Starter Review

Of all types of reviews, starter reviews are most important. I cannot stress this enough.

The reasons are two-fold:

1) If you don't take care of or don't want to arrange for getting starter reviews, you'll also have a hard time finding readers. Everything needs to be learned, including – finding readers.

2) Starter reviews influence sales in (a) giving readers a reason to buy and (b) setting the stage for getting more reviews that will influence getting future sales.

To illustrate this second element, let's go back in time.

On September 1, 1998, "Harry Potter and the Sorcerer's Stone" was released in the United States. The book received its first ten reviews on November 9, 16, 17, and 22, and December 6, 7, 9, 14, 23, and 25, 1998.

That's right. Since in 1998, very few people owned a personal computer, "Harry Potter and the Sorcerer's Stone" received its first online review only 70 days after the book was released. And, after that, it took 16 days until this bestseller received 10 online reviews.

In those days, publishers were skeptical about the success of online bookstores and no traditional publisher tried to influence getting reviews by marketing specifically to people who owned a computer. Books received online reviews totally by chance. Consequently, the first Harry Potter reviews are about as honest as can be. Four of these ten reviews were <u>perfect starter reviews</u>.

The very first reviewer pointed out that he or she was "looking for a non-sports book" for his/her ten year old child. He/she explained that the family was so delighted with the book that he/she shared the story with others, over the phone. (Remember, in 1998, there was no texting and no social media.) The reviewer ended on the note that they were looking for the sequel on the Internet.

The immensely strong argument in this very first review of "Harry Potter" is that the reviewer was looking for "a non-sports book for a ten-year-old." Indeed, not all American children enjoy playing football or soccer. And, maybe, secretly, some of these children want to be wizards. So, we can guess what parents thought when they read this review.

Additionally, the reviewer hinted that they knew that the sequel was out in Great Britain but not in the United States, hence they were trying to acquire it on the Internet. Today, that's a normal thought. Then, in 1998, making this statement demonstrated utter desperation, "We can't wait... We have to have this second book – NOW."

Reviewer #3 was nine-year-old Karen. She signed her review. It is titled "A book that keeps you reading!!!!!!!!!!!!" That's 12 exclamation marks.

There is nothing to add. Even as top reviewer who has collected hundreds of likes on individual book reviews, I know that I could never write a review that outshines the effort of a nine-year-old who had to share with the world that she loves this book.

Reviewer #5 mentioned that he/she bought the book on the advice of a clerk at a children's book store. He/she also stated that their son read most of "Harry Potter" alone because he was so excited about the book.

The obvious "sales arguments" are (a) an expert (the bookstore clerk) recommended this book and (b) the admission that the son read "Harry Potter" without having to be encouraged. The fact that the parent mentions it implies significance.

Reviewer #6 was a teenager who explained that he loved the descriptions of Harry Potter's sport Quidditch and that he wished that it was a real sport because it was a "mix of sorcery and basketball."

Can you see how these by-chance-reviews go full circle? Basically, these reviews are saying, "Whether your child likes sports or not, this book is such a great read that they'll read it alone, by themselves. If you buy this book, you are a great parent who encourages their child to read!

End of case!

These four by-chance-starter reviews reflected exactly what buyers needed to hear.

*

Why did I pick the example of starter reviews that were posted so far back? Because, then nobody pondered the significance of online reviews or tried influence getting best starter reviews.

Today, you can do something; you can influence the sales of your book by asking the *right* people to post starter reviews.

1

The best method is to try acquiring starter reviews even before you release your book. Doing that ensures that your book will have reviews as soon as it's listed for sale.

Therefore, send out ARCs (Advanced Reader Copies), mobi files or proof copies, to trusted, excellent reviewers who most likely will relate to your book because they have a personal interest in your book's content.

2

Do NOT aim for getting too many starter reviews; you don't need more than about half-a-dozen. The reason for this advice is: Since you provide the ARCs, these reviews will be listed as non-verified reviews.

Some things have changed since 1998. The publication of many blogs about fake reviews on ecommerce sites causes many consumers to value verified and non-verified reviews differently.

Please also make sure to remind ARC reviewers that they have to mention that they received a free copy of your book, in their review (as required per Amazon's community guidelines).

http://www.amazon.com/gp/community-help/customer-reviews-guidelines

3

Absolutely NEVER EVER tell anybody what to write because – they'll do it!!!

One facet of getting starter reviews is that readers share their personal thoughts, which ideally are very different.

Remember, one of Harry Potter's first reviewers mentioned that they were looking for "a non-sports book for a ten-year-old." Another one wished that Quidditch was a real sport, because he'd like to play it. Both of them, sports enthusiast or not, made their case why "Harry Potter and the Sorcerer's Stone" was *a great book for them.*

If J.K. Rowling would have been asked to come up with these arguments, she would not have been able to do it because at the time her oldest daughter was only five years old. Hence, Rowling couldn't not know how a ten year old whose parent isn't an author would react.

Therefore, always let reviewers bring their own, honest, heart-felt arguments. If you picked the right reviewers who have an interest in your book's content, I promise they'll come up with better arguments than you could ever formulate.

*

For example: If you penned a book about anything related to young children (story books, early childhood education books, parenting books), ask moms or grandmas to review your book. Forget that friend of yours who has a doctorate in English Literature from Harvard University (unless that person is a mom or a dad of a young child). Even the review from a professor of literature cannot possibly be as authentic, heartfelt, and involved as the review from a mom who writes something like, "The author writes a lot about ...xyz..., which is exactly what I experience with my 3-year old son..."

Please note that the professor of literature would probably write a much more stylish review than "the mom" or "the grandma", but "mom" and "grandma" can relate to the topic and have personal opinions about it.

*

The same goes for fiction books. Often, the authors of fantasy books are taken aback when I tell them that I do not read and review this genre. The truth is that I probably can't even write a good review of a fantasy novel.

Since I never read "Lord of the Rings" or any other famous fantasy novels, I have no education when it comes to this topic. Naturally, I could read a fantasy novel and compose a two sentence review, for instance,

> *"What an interesting fantasy world author XYZ created. I was stunned with his/her mesmerizing descriptions of (... pick three items from the book...) Couldn't put it down..."*

Any wordsmith can write this review, including me who just told you that I never read fantasy novels. I also don't need to read any book to write this. All I need is a copy of the book so I can look up the "three items from the book."

However, make no mistake, this type of review does not help in selling books because it does not contain a single element that could convince readers to buy.

On the other hand, this type of generic review sets the stage for more people posting this type of vacuous review. That's not ideal.

People follow patterns. If they see that, in bus station, everybody lines up, they'll line up too; if everybody is sitting on a bench, they'll look for a seat. And, if they see an overwhelming majority of 2-sentence reviews, they probably won't write a long in-depth review.

Maybe, right now you are thinking, "Great advice. I should have known this three years ago when I published my book."

Well, that's why you are reading *this* book.

In the words of George Eliot,

"It is never too late to be what you might have been."

and,

"The strongest principle of growth lies in the human choice."

George Eliot is the pen name of Mary Anne Evans, an English novelist, poet, journalist, translator, and a leading writer of the Victorian era. She used a male pen name to ensure that her works would be taken seriously.

Mary Ann Evans was creative about getting her work out in times when women writers were limited to writing lighthearted romance. These aren't your restraints. Today's authors' biggest problem is a saturated market.

Which is why, it is so important that your book is highlighted by insightful reviews.

So, don't bemoan lost opportunities but set out to get insightful reviews – right now!

The "Verified" Friend's, Fan's, and Follower's Review

Remember that I mentioned to not give out too many ARCs for starter reviews?

Your overall goal should be to get "verified reviews" from your friends and fans.

*

If a reader reviews a book he purchased on Amazon, this review will be marked as verified review. Amazon wants to indicate that they know for a fact that the reviewer purchased the book. Amazon's only limitation is that customers have to spend at least $50 at Amazon (for books and/or products) before they are allowed to post reviews.

Additionally, reviews of free books that were acquired during a 5-free-days promo will be listed as verified reviews.

To take advantage of this second option, you have to enroll your book in Amazon's Kindle KDP Select program.

The negative aspect of this second option is that when customers who are enrolled in Amazon's Kindle Unlimited program read your book for free during *the remaining 85 days* of the enrollment period, these reviews will be registered as non-verified reviews.

In short, while you can use Amazon's Kindle KDP Select program to boost your readership, there might also be a backlash. During 85 of 90 days per enrollment period, your book might collect too many non-verified reviews.

To bypass this issue, you could follow a step-by-step plan.

First, offer your book at reduced price for pre-order so your friends, fans, and followers are motivated to buy your new book right away. This will help you to get verified, trusted fan reviews. If you don't want to offer your book for pre-order, offer it at a reduced price for one week to achieve the same effect.

Once your book acquired a few dozen reviews, it might be a great idea to enroll it in Amazon's KDP Select program to gain new fans.

Remember that accumulating book reviews follows the "law of attraction". Hence, if you announce or advertise, "Get this mystery novel with 55 reviews averaging 4.5***** free," you will achieve much better results than if you offered your book for free when it features only a few reviews.

*

Many authors try to follow a similar course of action by offering their book in a review club, accumulating anywhere from six to two dozen reviews and then advertise their book on Twitter.

It's not the same concept.

Friends, fans, and followers are people who know you and your work.

They are also people who can write insightful reviews because they really know you and/or your work.

For instance, when my friends and fans are being asked to describe my work, they'll say, "Gisela writes naked, no-fluff books for authors and most recently also the Little Blue Book series for authors."

I also wrote two award-winning life skills book, but (unfortunately) that's not the work I am known for.

To put further proof to my statement, I will also reveal what many of my close friends know. I own a pen name author Twitter account. Many dozens of my friends and followers follow this account which tweets all day long. This pen name author also wrote a great book which received a few 5-star reviews. Even though the book has been on free promotion a few times, not one of my friends and followers read and reviewed it.

Just tweeting, "My book is free" to "every reader out there" leads to very limited results.

*

In short: Though Internet book marketers will propose various ways to "achieve your dream" of becoming a bestselling author, the truth is achieving a dream takes hard work. You can't buy it. In addition to writing a good book, building a fan base is an essential part of becoming a well-known author.

Therefore, network on social media platforms, blog, write guest articles, attend live writers' club meetings, local library's author meetings, and do whatever you must do to build a fan base. The only other option to build a fan base is to dazzle Goodreads readers with your story writing skills. (My other identity can't do that because it would lift my cover.)

The Review Club Review

During the last six to ten months, Internet marketers have taken a foothold in book marketing. Many of them offer book review clubs.

The obvious reason is: Internet marketers are very aware of the effects of great reviews because the effect is the same for any kind of product – from books to backyard furniture.

There are two types of review clubs – the ones which offer books for free in order to gain reviews quickly and the ones where authors have to buy and review a book before they can introduce their own book so other members may buy and review it.

Technically, the second option is a violation of Amazon's community guidelines because these guidelines forbid offering any kind of incentive. Please see details at:

http://www.amazon.com/gp/community-help/customer-reviews-guidelines

It has to be all of our best guess if Amazon's algorithm can filter out these reviews and if, in the future, they might delete them.

The first option, to try accumulating reviews quickly by offering the book to other members for free should be used sparingly because it could lead to too many non-verified reviews.

The most extreme example I have seen was the second book from an author whose first novel (same genre) received only three reviews. Most surprisingly, this author's second book received forty-one reviews. None of the books were listed in Amazon KDP Select.

This discrepancy had me startled. How could it be that none of the second book's reviewers were interested in reading and reviewing the author's first book? Especially, since all of them had awarded the second book with 4-star or 5-star reviews.

A simple check revealed the facts: I first clicked "See all reviews" of the second book. Next, I set Amazon's pull-down menu to "verified purchase only" and could see at one glance that the second book had received only two verified reviews.

****

Side note:
Amazon's installment of the pull-down menu is probably also a reaction to cheating efforts and accumulating reviews via review exchanges.

Until March 2016, this pull-down menu did not exist. Consumers had to count verified and non-verified reviews, often having to look at many pages. Typically, Amazon features around 10 reviews per page. Which means that consumers would have had to look at five pages to count the verified and non-verified reviews of the mentioned book.

If a book had more than 100 reviews (10 pages), this process could take a while and probably very few consumers did it.

That's why before March 2016, "reviewing each others' books" seemed to make sense, and Internet marketers promoted this method to such an extent that apparently it caused Amazon to install the pull-down menu.

Trying to outsmart a data hoarder like Amazon just does not work.

****

Getting back to the book with forty-one reviews of which only two were verified reviews: Almost all the non-verified reviews featured the annotations, "I received an advanced reader copy of this book..." and also "I was given a free review copy in exchange..."

To me, it looked as if the author had *wised up* after not receiving too many reviews for his/her first book hence the author made sure this would not happen again.

But, is this effort going to help in selling the book?

Or to put it more bluntly, do you think that thirty-nine non-verified reviews of a total of forty-one reviews will convince readers to rush and buy this book?

*

If this author would have asked me for advice, I would have said,

1. Do NOT publish the second book before you exhaust the options your first book offers.

2. Offer the first book for free and try building your fan base.

3. If you already wrote the second book, you have it easy to say, "Subscribe here to learn about ..." or "My next book is going to be released soon..."

4. Also, if you really must engage in review exchanges, for heaven's sake, use the first book!

5. There is no faster way to say that something isn't quite right than an explosive reaction that can't be easily explained. If, indeed, the readers of the second book were so enthused about it, at least 25% (ten reviewers) should have also wanted to read this author's first book.

*

What if results aren't this extreme?

I personally have seen half-a-dozen books with two or three verified reviews and seven to nine non-verified reviews; in each case, the non-verified reviews outnumbered the verified reviews by at least 3:1.

It's anybody's guess what real readers think when they see these numbers but one issue could cause problems.

As all of us know, it is a fact that a good percentage of authors try to cheat. This enrages other authors who spill the beans and share their thoughts in blogs and Youtube videos.

These blogs get shared. In 2017, one of the harshest blogs was shared 1,440 times. Combined, the shared blogs reached millions of people. The clear message was, "Authors cheat on Amazon."

Additionally, in 2017, StockNews.com and even Bloomberg reported about efforts to cheat on Amazon.

Does reading these articles and blogs make consumers think twice about believing non-verified reviews?

Already, in 2016, Fortune magazine advised to "put more weight on reviews with the "Amazon Verified Purchase" tag."

http://fortune.com/2016/03/14/paid-amazon-reviews/

*

I wrote three blogs advising against overusing review clubs in October 2016. The reason why I was certain that Amazon would do something about this situation was that on October 3, 2016 Amazon banned product vendors from offering a free product in exchange for an "incentivized review."

Years of observing Amazon taught me that whenever Amazon changes the community guidelines for product vendors, usually they change the community guidelines for authors three to six months later.

Indeed, five months later, Amazon introduced the pull-down menu which makes it easy to see how many reviews are verified and non-verified.

The reality of running an ecommerce business is that corporations have to ensure that the FTC's (Federal Trade Commission) truth-in-advertising laws are being honored. Consequently, tens of thousands of authors posting reviews of other authors' books present some problems.

Personally, I believe that Amazon's team sees these problems exactly the same way as indie authors do, which is why they have done their best to funnel readers into Goodreads.

The ecommerce giant acquired Goodreads, the social media platform for readers, in 2013. Goodreads isn't an ecommerce platform but a social media platform like Facebook; consequently, the FTC's truth-in-advertising laws don't have to be enforced as on an ecommerce platform.

The Goodreads Review

In authors' groups I often get to hear that Goodreads reviewers are mean. Though it is true that at one time Goodreads was overrun by trolls, after Amazon purchased Goodreads they changed the Goodreads User Guidelines in September 2013. Ad hominem attacks, off-topic comments about a reader or author, as well as trolling are specific reasons for Goodreads deleting reviews that contain these violations as well as taking other appropriate actions.

https://www.goodreads.com/topic/show/1499741-important-note-regarding-reviews

Naturally, Goodreads enforces their guidelines, just like Amazon enforces theirs.

The most obvious reasons why Goodreads is the best social media platform for authors to network and seek reviews are:

1. Amazon has been funneling readers into Goodreads since 2013. Goodreads has now more than 65 million members/readers.
   https://www.statista.com/statistics/252986/number-of-registered-members-on-goodreadscom/
2. Goodreads members focus on reading, books, and authors. Nobody is there to rant about politics or share cute kitten videos.
3. If, on an average day, you have only between one and four hours to network, Goodreads is the most efficient venue to spend your time.
4. On Goodreads, readers volunteer to beta-read books, discuss books, offer personal insights, which are all activities that will help you to become a better writer.
5. On Goodreads, you can actually see who reads your book. Amazon never told you that.

6. In contrast to Amazon where consumers have to spend $50.00 before they can post a review, there are no such requirements on Goodreads.
7. Whereas Amazon disconnected their reviewers' email addresses you can reach most Goodreads readers and reviewers.
8. In contrast to Amazon that only lists top reviewers Goodreads shows authors their top users, top readers, top reviewers, most popular reviewers, and much more.
9. If you go through the relatively minor trouble of planning an event, online or offline, Goodreads allows you to inform all your friends and followers. You can use this option to boost sales. Again, Amazon never gave authors the option to reach their books' buyers.

It's obvious that Amazon builds out Goodreads to once and for all own the readers' market, US-wide and possibly the International markets, too.

And, if you need any more reason to be there:
Stephen King (2544 friends), Cassandra Clare (1347 friends), Neil Gaiman (5435 friends), James Patterson (554 friends), John Green (691 friends), Dan Brown (1828 friends), John Grisham (2415 friends), Nora Roberts (1 friend), Khaled Hosseini (3826 friends), Charlaine Harris (312 friends), E.L. James (4879 friends), and Margaret Atwood (72 friends) are there, too.

It seems many of these really famous authors used the platform to network and to get reviews... what else?

https://www.goodreads.com/author/on_goodreads

Additionally, you can use your Goodreads links to market your books on any other social media platform, like so:

Your author profile

https://www.goodreads.com/author/show/1009368.Gisela_Hausmann

and even your links to specific books

https://www.goodreads.com/book/show/36291472-naked-good-reads

Personally, I find that posting Goodreads links on Twitter works better than posting short links or Amazon links. Probably, when readers see Goodreads links they don't feel pressured to buy.

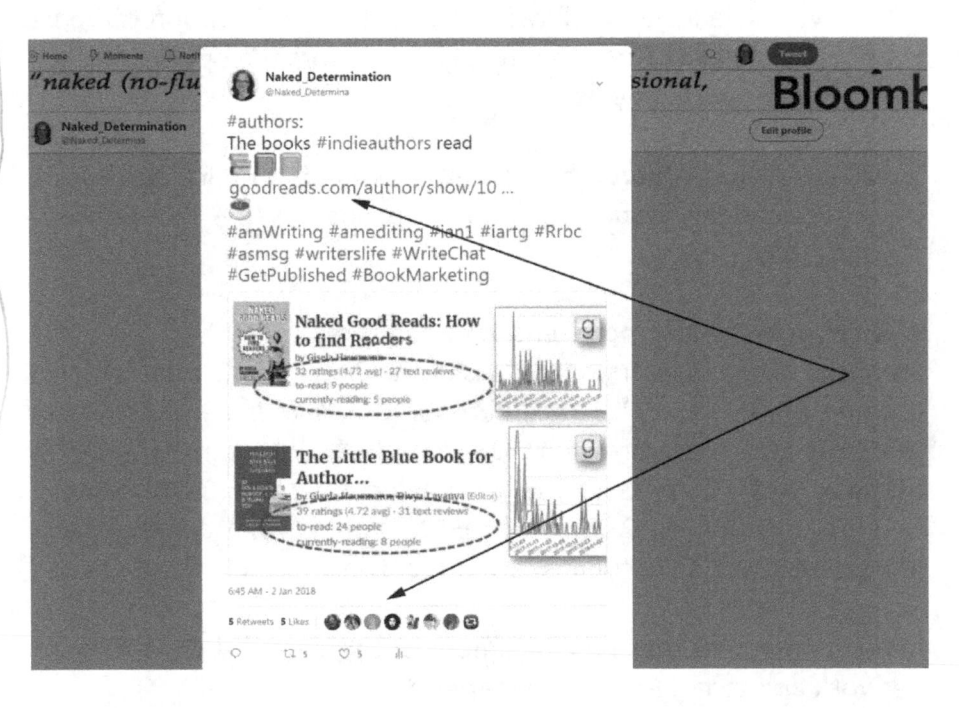

Lastly, if you want public libraries to acquire your book, Goodreads reviews are more important than Amazon reviews. WorldCat is the world's largest library catalog, helping librarians find library materials online. WorldCat features only Goodreads and librarians' reviews but not Amazon reviews.

Example: My book "Naked News" features 17 reviews on Goodreads and 53 reviews on Amazon, none of which are visible on WorldCat, only the Goodreads reviews are visible.

http://www.worldcat.org/title/naked-news-for-indie-authors-how-not-to-invest-your-marketing/oclc/957559481

To find your links to Worldcat go to your book(s)' Goodreads page(s) and search for the link "Libraries" right below your book's blurb.

Regular Customer Reviews

Amazon recommends that reader/reviewers write about six sentences. That's a manageable task. Having studied thousands of reviews, I have found that the only thing that influences the quality of future reviews from regular customers who may have never heard about you before they read your book is the quality of your book's already existing reviews. If three of four reviews retell your book's plot, many of the following reviews will state something similar.

On the other hand, if the top-rated review says, "OMG! I sooo love this book. Samantha and Sebastian's love story is just so beautiful I drooled over ..." this review will encourage other readers "to open up" and reveal what they drooled about.

Though no professional reviewer would use this kind of wording, it is exactly the kind of review that sells thousands of books, maybe even more books than the New York Times Book Review.

Hence, if your book doesn't feature emotionally charged reviews – Get them! (Remember – No cheating though! If suddenly, after the release of this book 10,000 reviews that state "I drooled over..." pop up on Amazon, you can bet ten bucks that Amazon will notice.)

Book Signing Event Attendees' reviews

Especially since I stressed the importance of acquiring verified reviews it may sound strange that I also advocate to seek reviews from readers who buy your book at live book signings or other speaking events. Obviously, the attendees can't post verified reviews.

Meeting real readers in person is important because they won't forget you; they are also more likely to tell their friends about meeting you. Building personal connections with real readers encourages *original* word-of-mouth marketing.

If you are not "famous" yet, you should try to arrange for book signings at small local bookstores. People who visit local bookstores to buy books or have coffee there, instead of shopping at Amazon or drinking coffee at Starbucks, will also be inclined to support a local author because "shopping local" is part of their life philosophy.

Therefore:

1. Bring double-sided business cards that also feature one excerpt from a review. Give a card to everybody you meet.

2. Show interest in your visitors. Ask them what kind of books they read. If you get them to share personal information you'll have it easier to get personal yourself and say something like, "Please don't forget to post an online review. As you can see, there are thousands of books (make a sweeping gesture pointing at the store's shelves) and there are even more books online. The only way indie authors like me even have a chance to score in this market is if our books receive reviews."

3. Then pause to see if the buyer has questions about the reviewing process like, "I never know what to write."

5-6 Sentences

4. If buyers ask you this question, suggest "Oh, this is easy. There is no need to retell the story like for a book report. Please just write (a) what you liked best about my book, or (b) what surprised you about my book."

5. Your goal is to make readers who may have never reviewed a book feel comfortable about this task.

*

Sometimes, you'll be rewarded with unexpected surprises.

> *"... All the facts you need to know. I met the author at a local library during her presentation...she doesn't exaggerate... "*

This sentence is part of a verified review of one of my books. It looks like the author listened to one of my presentations, went home, and purchased my book on Amazon. He or she also told the world that we met in person.

Even a non-verified review of a reader who did not purchase your book on Amazon adds credibility if the buyer writes, "... I met author ..xyz... at a book signing. She is... "

This type of review is a special review that will tell consumers a lot about you as a person.

Real Life Author Group Member's reviews

If you have never attended a real life author or reader group-meeting you'll be surprised to feel these groups' buzzing energy.

People who attend real life meetings have to get dressed, drive to the meeting place, and often fulfill some requirements like reading a book in a specific time frame, and also purchase a beverage at the meeting place. People who do all of this regularly are doers!

The second advantage of "connecting with people at life meetings" is that not even Amazon's mighty algorithm can detect what you discuss at such occasions.

So, check out what's going on at your local library. Most public libraries host book clubs. Also check out Meet-up groups.

The largest Meetup group I occasionally visit has 500+ members. The smallest group to which I have spoken has 26 members.

To give you an impression of what you awaits you if you decide to do the same, please see this list of smaller U.S. cities I picked in random. The number in brackets indicates the number of writers and readers groups within a 25-mile radius.

Albuquerque, NM (7)
Billings, MT (1)
Birmingham, AL (3)
Carson City, NV (5)
Kansas City, KS (6)
Providence, RI (8)
Syracuse, NY (2)
Tallahassee, FL (3)
Wilmington, NC (2)

There are even more opportunities if you live close to a big city like Chicago, IL that offers 48 writers and readers groups to choose from.

At all Meetup meetings I attended, members were interested in buying and reading my books. Group members buy books because they want to learn about your writing style, how you format your book, or they want to start a mutually beneficial relationship. Maybe they are looking for a mentor.

Additionally, I also found that people who meet an author *in person* will recommend your book to others because they have a personal connection. Whereas on-line contacts really cannot do much else but share postings into an endless stream of information, people you meet in real life share information via word-of-mouth.

It's an incredibly effective method. I have received countless emails from people who emailed me, "I got your contact information from ...xyz... who heard you speaking at ..." Therefore, make sure that your book includes all of your contact information and always bring business cards to every meeting.

Lastly, if you can't find a Meetup group in your region, consider starting your own!

For more information please check out: https://www.meetup.com/

https://www.meetup.com/cities/**gb/**
https://www.meetup.com/cities/**fr/**
https://www.meetup.com/cities/**de/**
https://www.meetup.com/cities/**at/**
https://www.meetup.com/cities/**it/**
https://www.meetup.com/cities/**au/**

For Meetup groups in other countries please google.

The Top Reviewer's or Hall of Fame Reviewer's Review

As a group, Amazon top reviewers have a special status. They write the reviews Amazon consumers like *best*.

The reviews of the current top-5 reviewers have been liked 67,422 times, on average.

The reviews of the five reviewers who achieved Hall-of-Fame reviewer ranking most often have been liked 71,939 times, on average.

Typically, top reviewers write seven paragraph reviews which most authors like better than Kirkus' reviews.

*

As mentioned before, unfortunately, Amazon disconnected the top reviewers' email addresses. This was a hard blow for indie authors. To my knowledge, Amazon was the only ecommerce store that gave authors (and product vendors) access to their 10,000 top reviewers.

That being said, maybe you still have top reviewers' email addresses because they reviewed one of your books in the past. If a top reviewer liked one of your books he or she might be interested in reading your next book, too.

To approach top reviewers correctly, put yourself in the top reviewer's shoes. It is no secret that top reviewers' ranks improve with the number of likes their reviews receive. Hence, always like every positive review. If you don't it'll appear as if you don't value the reviewer's effort.

The second truth is that since many consumers don't want to check out non-verified reviews, top reviewers prefer to write verified reviews.

Consequently, your chances to get your book accepted improve if you offer your book to top reviewers when you have it on a 5-days-free-promo. Doing this allows the reviewer to post a verified review.

When contacting a top reviewer never forget to mention if your book is on a free promotion.

If you get lucky, a top reviewer who trusts that your book is a great read might even acquire it during a 99 cents promotion.

Please note my words "if the reviewer trusts ..." This means you have to present your case in a proper and sensible way.

Most top reviewers read so many books that they can tell by your review request if you are a great writer, or — not. They see your review request as a writing sample. If you don't apply yourself or quickly tailor a template of a review request, your chances of getting your book reviewed by a top reviewer are almost zero.

Top reviewers receive many review requests, hence "judging" the writer's email writing skills helps in picking the "best book."

Also, never write BS like, "... I would also be willing to send you my book as a gift so you don't have to purchase it! ..." (This is a much abused line from many real review requests.)

Every top reviewer knows where to find free books and they also know that Kirkus charges $425 for writing a review. Therefore, this sentence sounds either silly or insulting, depending on the mood of the reviewer.

Negative Reviews

- "Haters gotta hate."

- "Personally, I don't leave bad reviews."

- My grandmother said, "If you have nothing nice to say, don't say anything at all."

Statements like these are being thrown around in every indie author forum.

They ignore human's desire of wanting *to learn*.

- Wanting to learn means to understand that no matter how good we are there is always room for improvement.

- Wanting to learn means to use individual little clues to understand what we could do, specifically, to reach the famous "next level."

The naked truth is that over the last few years, things have gotten a lot easier for people who want to learn.

Only twenty years ago, authors would have never heard from real readers until they became famous enough to receive readers' fan mail (or hate mail), via snail mail.

Instead, aspiring authors had to clear the hurdle of getting accepted by an agent and also a traditional publisher.

While there is no need to rehash well-known anecdotes of publishers' failures to recognize future bestsellers, one thing needs to be pointed out: When authors receive rejection letters, most often they don't learn <u>why</u> their books got rejected.

Maybe, the book isn't any good, maybe the publisher doesn't want to publish a book of this genre, or one of another hundred reasons.

Since, typically, publishing houses send generic letters which equate to the word "no," the author doesn't know what they could do to reach the next level.

In contrast, about half of all negative reviews contain at least a kernel of truth.

Also, considering the many articles and blogs about fake reviews, consumers get suspicious if they see only glorious reviews. Everybody knows that not everybody likes every product the same.

On Amazon even books from Nobel laureates in Literature receive 1-star reviews. Hemingway's *The Old Man and the Sea* received one hundred and thirty-five 1-star reviews (or 6 percent of all reviews) and John Steinbeck's *The Grapes of Wrath* received ninety-seven 1-star reviews (or 5 percent of all reviews), as of January 1, 2018.

Professional writers know that, ignore negative comments, and move on. It takes a thick skin to make it to the top.

Troll Reviews

A troll review is not just a negative review; per definition, its aim is to provoke other online users into an emotional response often for the troll's own amusement.

Hence, never respond!
Don't give trolls what they looking for, they don't deserve to get satisfaction that somebody noticed their efforts.

From a technical point of view I hate troll reviews. I became an expert in online reviews because I believe that online reviews are the greatest invention since PCs became widely available.

As long as trolls and fake reviewers can be kept in check, consumers get an opportunity to find out why others liked or disliked a particular product. At the same time, sellers get feedback from actual customers.

Hence, I also believe that all corporations who run online platforms should do everything possible to block trolls. However, that is not happening.

I personally complained to Amazon about receiving two reviews from an obvious troll (reviewer ranking #54,600,000+) who posted thirty-five 1-star and two 2-star reviews among the sixty reviews she penned to date.

Though this "reviewer" also posted verified reviews, all her 1-star and 2-star reviews are non-verified reviews. This "coincidence" would even prompt my sweet grandmother to say, "Something isn't right with this."

However, Amazon did not remove the reviews. I take comfort in the fact that one has to "be somebody" to attract the attention of a troll.

Let's face it – Everybody from Steven Seagal to President Trump and from Kim Kardashian to Hillary Clinton is getting trolled. Consequently, if you are getting trolled, obviously you reached the first level of getting famous.

Additionally, just having one or two trolls reviews can actually help business.

Here are one illustration and two questions for you:

Which one of these two books would you look at first?
and
Which review would you look at first?

Customer reviews			Customer reviews		
★★★★☆ 38			★★★★☆ 38		
4.6 out of 5 stars ▾			4.6 out of 5 stars ▾		
5 star		71%	5 star		71%
4 star		26%	4 star		26%
3 star		0%	3 star		0%
2 star		0%	2 star		0%
1 star		3%	1 star		0%

While the presence of one or a few negative reviews confirms that the author is exposing their book to real readers, an obvious troll review signals that the author has enough "star power" to attract trolls.

In the 21st century, apparently, that's good thing.

Too short reviews

In general, consumers don't like too short reviews because there is nothing be learned from mini-reviews like "Great!" or "I loved this book."

That being said, your book needs these reviews too, but they should not set the tone.

Every book should have up to 10% short reviews just because people are used to seeing them.

*

5-10% Neg.

10% Short/worthless but ⊕

35%   4 ☆

45%   5 ☆

Getting to work

To reach a goal, you must have a goal.
The better you define your goal, the faster you'll reach it.
Therefore, before you get to work, check out your "competition."
In sports terms: You can't score higher if you don't know what the score is.

Clear your browser history or access Amazon from a computer you don't use too often, type your genre into the search field, and check what Amazon is showing you. Then, compare the reviews of bestsellers with "others" and, of course, with your own book(s).

Now, you can get to work!

If your book doesn't have too many reviews yet, immediately aim for getting excellent starter reviews. Find people who are interested in your topic, your material, your style... your brand. *only 5 or 6* ①

If your book has "insufficient" reviews or only reviews of a certain ② type (unemotional, too short, too much retelling of the plot, etc.), find people who are passionate about your topic, your material, your style... your brand. *need 10 to 25 verified*

Please don't come back and tell me that you already did this. If you only network in Facebook authors' groups, you haven't really looked for readers and reviewers, yet.

1. Stop hanging out on Facebook pursuing the same people over and again.
2. Pick up the phone and call your friends and acquaintances. Today, calling somebody has almost the same effect as seventy years ago when only few people had a telephone. Once again, receiving a phone call means "This is important." *Network*

3. Gift two to three copies of your book to colleagues who told you that they like to read. Don't forget to dedicate the books. If you don't have this kind of information, use your time at the water cooler wisely.
4. Find out if your local library has a writers or readers group and register... Also, go there!
5. Find one, two, three local Meet-up groups for writers and visit them; typically they meet every two to three weeks.
6. Visit a small independent book store, in person, and schedule a book signing.
7. Fix up your Goodreads profile and start networking there. If you want to score a bestseller, you can't escape this task. The site has 65 million members; one in ten Americans is there.

Always remember – Your book needs diversity of opinions!

Two of Harry Potter's first fans were kids on opposite ends of the spectrum. One didn't like sports and the other one loved sports so much that he wanted to ride on a broom, trying to catch a fast flying, buzzing golden ball the size of a golf ball, while possibly getting knocked off the broom by either a competitor or a heavy leather ball the size of a football.

It is unlikely that you attract this diversity of readers if you network mostly with other authors. The two completely opposing opinions from authors are "well-written" and "the book needs editing." Because, that's what writers write.
Writers look at books from a writer's perspective.

To "get to the next level," [more readers] you also need reviews from people who only read two or three books per year.

Ever read some of the reviews of "Fifty Shades of Grey"? They feature opinions from readers who had never even contemplated the concept of bondage as well as of hard-core BDSM fans.

Here are 3 truths:

Your book cannot reach bestseller status without attracting large numbers of people who have different opinions, skills, knowledge, backgrounds, and so on.

Your book cannot reach bestseller status without you facing your critics. Consequently, it might be a better strategy to face them early and see if you can turn some of them into friends and fans.

Your book cannot reach bestseller status without you looking for new readers every day!

Authors' communication skills

Overall, authors' communication skills seem to have eroded over the last three years.

In 2015, I published the first edition of this book. It went on to become a 2015 Kindle Book Awards Finalist, one of five books in the overall genre Non-fiction.

The book was first released at a time when every author could still contact one of roughly 5,000 Amazon top reviewers who reviewed indie books at the time.

In this first edition, I pointed out three majorly important factors:

1. Study the reviewer's profile and explain in your own words why your book is a perfect fit. (At the same time I also advised not to use templates because top reviewers who receive a lot of requests emails know all commonly used templates by heart.)
2. Do not treat top reviewers as part of Amazon's inventory because they are not.
3. Tell people who you want to review your book something they haven't heard yet.

The 2015 and 2016 editions offered insights that helped authors in gaining reviews from top reviewers very quickly. The author who to my knowledge "scored" the best was able to gain 16 reviews from top reviewers, in just one month. Top reviewers listened up when these properly written emails landed in their Inboxes.

In the meantime, so many books have been and are getting published that these communication skills have to be applied even when talking with your friends and acquaintances.

Here is the data about ISBN numbers assigned to self publishing authors; please note, they do not include the ISBN numbers Amazon, Createspace, and other publishers make available.

https://www.statista.com/statistics/605067/isbn-self-published-books/

This means that probably all your friends who read voraciously have more than one friend who writes books. Plus, all of them know where to find free books.

Still, the tighter and tougher the market gets, the more it seems authors' communication skills have fallen by the wayside.

Here are a few examples:

In general, authors don't explain anymore why they think their book is a perfect fit for a reader, not even to social media friends. Instead, they argue, "My book is free."

Well, so are more than 60,000 other books, on any given day, which is why word "free" isn't necessarily a great argument.

When a few months ago, I offered my book, *"The Little Blue Book for Authors: 53 Dos & Don'ts Nobody Is Telling You"* (30 pages) free for five days, quite many author friends responded with "I'll accept your book for review, when can I send you mine?"

Since my book has only 30 pages and theirs 300+ pages, I have to assume these authors did not even look at the details of my book but offered review trading, automatically. Instead of pointing out what's great about their book, they just wanted "to trade."

That's a really bad habit; generally speaking, review trading does not lead to receiving great reviews.

Authors also keep referring to their book as "my book." *In this market, how is anybody supposed to know what kind of book the one or other author wrote?*

I am betting twenty bucks that fifty percent of all Americans can't even name both of Harper Lee's only two published novels.

In the mentioned Little Blue Book, I offered the following advice:

*

Never, ever refer to your book as "my book." It means giving away a marketing opportunity.

- weak:

"... if you wanted to review *my book.*"

- better:

"... if you wanted to review *my romance novel.*"

- best:

"...if you wanted to review *my romance novel telling the story of an 18th century monk who falls in love with one of Queen Mary Antoinette's ladies-in-waiting who turns out to be a spy for Russian Empress Catherine the Great.*"

This last description not only allows a potential reader to make an educated decision if they want to read the book, it will also arouse interest in people who like love stories, complicated scenarios (monks aren't supposed to fall in love), history, and even spy stories.

*

Sometimes, it seems to me as if car salesmen and real-estate agents are more creative in pointing out their "goods' positive elements" than authors.

Especially real-estate agents demonstrate immense talents when it comes to choosing "best wording."

A "cozy apartment" is an apartment not much bigger than a walk-in closet. "Updated!" means that somebody painted the walls. "Vintage details" is a codeword for "this real estate object is really old (and drafty)".

WHY aren't authors doing the same? They are supposed to be the wordsmiths.

***

In all honesty, I believe that one reason why authors have such a hard time finding reviewers is that, overall, they do not sufficiently communicate their book's qualities.

It's human nature to reject any unspecific offer that does not explain *why* the buyer should buy.

You can observe this behavior in any supermarket. There are the little elderly ladies who offer taste samples to every customer who walks by their stand.

"Want to try our guacamole?"

"Sure."

(Munch... munch... "Mm! Mm! Good!")

"Guacamole is only $2.99 today, it's fifty percent off."

"Thank you, but not today!"

This exact dialog is going down probably in 50,000 supermarkets nationwide, while I am writing this.

The truth is that the supermarkets don't offer free guacamole samples because they want shoppers to buy guacamole. In reality, the supermarkets want to establish relationships that will lead to their shoppers not wandering off to "the other supermarket" five miles down the road but to always come back and shop where they get free guacamole samples.

This marketing concept helps supermarkets to sell more products than they'd if they focused on selling guacamole.

It is the equivalent of you blogging. When you blog, you are giving your fan community little samples of your work to hinder them from "wandering off."

If the supermarket really wanted to sell guacamole, the little elderly ladies would offer a sample and then ask, "Do you eat guacamole often? Do your children like it?"

The concept is: Demonstrating personal interest while at the same time encouraging the customer to focus on their need for guacamole.

When asked if the family likes guacamole, most people will think about this specific question. After answering, many people will decide to buy because the question reminded them that their wife, husband, or oldest daughter really likes guacamole, a lot.

The same is done in every nail salon and hair salon in the United States where employees ask their clients for the names of children and grand children they might never see, and so on.

Which brings me back to indie authors.

In all honesty, I cannot remember the last time an author introduced their book to me with an only remotely exciting description.

I also don't remember that anybody told me that they met so-and-so who told an exciting story that prompted them to check out or buy a book.

It seems to me that this is the result of authors getting overwhelmed with advice that book marketing can be automatized and/or or that tweeting the same advertisement again and again will lead to great sales results.

It won't.
If you need any proof for this statement, please pay attention to sales emails offering Twitter ad services.

Pretty much every Internet book marketer offers Twitter ads at a reduced price, up to 50% off.
Now, why is that?

"Looks good" vs. "This is what I have been looking for"

When I published my first ebook "Naked Determination: 41 Stories About Overcoming Fear" in 2012, I enrolled it in Amazon KDP Unlimited and put it on a free promo for five days. I did not buy any ads, I only posted on Facebook. When I woke up on the first day of the promotion, 600 copies had been pulled – just like so.

Then, in the early days of ebook publishing, the relatively few people who owned a Kindle knew where to go to find free ebooks. Also, a lot less ebooks were getting published.

In those days, the word "free" was good enough to spark interest.

From 2007 to 2013, Kindle owners bought ebooks that "looked good."

Today, it's a whole different ballgame. In reality, nobody is searching for a "good looking book." Readers want to buy books they "have been looking for."

Therefore, when seeking readers and reviewers always remember that you are looking for your specific market.

If you try to market "a love story," you are competing with 34% of all authors.

On the other hand, if you try to market a love story between two environmentalists, you are courting a very specific audience – people who are seeking love stories and value protecting the environment. By "zooming in" on your target audience, you are eliminating a lot of competition.

Additionally, you may even attract environmentalists who typically spend their time reading about today's environmental problems but might <u>also</u> enjoy reading some light-hearted content – a love story – **if** this book also addresses the topic "environment," which they care about a lot.

Just like Harry Potter's fans who knew other kids who wanted to be wizards, these people know other environmentalists who might also enjoy reading your book. Even more importantly, the environmentalists who read your "specific love story" will talk about it.

The same goes for mystery/crime novels or thrillers. Some people just don't care about bank robberies but they care a lot about illegal whale hunting and similar crimes.

Therefore, stop shouting "My book is free" to people who buy books that "look good." They aren't going to do anything for you because they'll grab every free book that "looks good."

Instead, define your specific target audience and present to them "the book they have been looking for."

More About Building a Fan Base

Writing teachers will tell you that you should never attempt to write for "everybody" but write for a specific reader or group of readers; in other words "Don't write for five year old children" or even for "five old girls" but write for a specific target group, for instance "five year old girls who want to become ballerinas."

(a) Vague definition of the reader base:
five to six year old children

(b) Better definition:
five to six year old girls

(c) Very specific definition:
five year old girls who want to become ballerinas.

The writing teachers' concept is that having a specific reader in mind will make your writing better because you'll describe situations and carve out elements your reader wants to know.

A good example is Barbara Park's famous children's book series "Junie B. Jones." Junie B. Jones frequently uses incorrect grammar and verbiage; for instance, she always calls fellow kindergartener Grace "that Grace."

"Junie B. Jones' adventures" are appealing to children who may feel insecure about going to school, don't really like their teachers, don't always get along with all classmates, and similar kindergarten situations. Millions of parents who see their children having these issues purchased the Junie B. Jones series.

Because Junie B. Jones constantly uses incorrect grammar, many parents and teachers also *did not* appreciate the series. From 2000-2009 the series was listed #71 on the American Library Association's list of the Top 100 Banned or Challenged Books.

Still, the series sold over 60 million copies.

***

Other bestsellers too sold millions of books though book critics dispraised them.

Among them are Stephanie Meyer's "Twilight", Dan Brown's "The Da Vinci Code," and E L James "Fifty Shades of Grey."

In reality, millions of readers don't care about the opinions of the American Library Association or famous book reviewers; they are simply looking for <u>the books they want to read</u>.

Books sell when "ideal customers/readers" spread word about the book they like.

When "ideal readers" share their enthusiasm, they even sway "non believers" to reconsider their opinions and buy these books.

I personally heard a first-grade teacher say, "If reading Junie B. Jones books encourages children to read, we'll read them. We can deal with the grammar later. The main goal is to get children to like reading books."

*

So, where does this leave you?

If you define your "perfect reader" and market <u>only to this group,</u> you have a better chance of scoring a bestseller than if you pay for Twitter ads marketing your book to a vaguely defined, huge reader base.

*

Example illustration: Though many girls and even some boys will read a story about little ballerinas, the three girls with the colored dresses are the ones

1. who are most likely going to **love** the book
2. who are most likely going to **tell** their friends about the book
3. whose moms are most likely going to **buy** the book
4. whose moms are most likely going to **spread the word** how much their daughters love the book, and
5. whose moms are most likely going to **review** the book.

*

Luckily, in November 2017, Twitter doubled the character limit for tweets to 280. Which gives you the opportunity to choose more hashtags to describe your book to the "perfect audience."

Here are some of the hashtags Junie B. Jones' books garnered.

#juniebjones
#studenttweet
#familyfun
#forthekids
#favoritebookseries
#spiritweek
#cutiepie
#summerreading
#firstchapterbook
#BookLoversDay
#readingiscool
#MustRead
#bookcharacterday
#oldtimesake
#usckidlit
#ChildrensBooks
#bannedbooksweek2017

*

If you had never heard about Junie B. Jones and you would discover the series because you were scanning Twitter for any one of these hashtags, you probably would look up the book series on Amazon. Even if you weren't looking for these hashtags they'd tell you why others love them.

And, that's how readers will find your book among the hundreds of thousands of books that will be published in 2018.

*

So, take a piece of paper and a pencil and define your perfect reader. Then, choose hashtags that describe your book to this specific audience.

Also, start experimenting with hashtags to see which ones work best, for your book.

Best of all – this is free.

Plus, the readers who find your book will be happy to pay anywhere from 99 cents to $3.99 for reading the works from an author who wrote a book "just for them."

Just like Junie B. Jones' fans, Anastasia Steele's fans, and Harry Potter's fans, fans of your book will also spread the word for you because you wrote "the book they were looking for."

Spread enthusiasm, passionately!

Last but not least - Protect your mindset, boost your spirits, and share your enthusiasm with others!

If you stumble over a Facebook discussion of a negative topic like "I just got the meanest, nastiest 1-star review" or "My book sales are way down. What about you?" DO NOT READ the entire discussion and do not comment. It will influence your mindset – negatively.

Instead, leave the group discussion immediately and change scenery. Head over to Twitter or Goodreads. Alternatively, don a nice suit and visit a local bookstore to ask if they'd be interested in hosting a book signing.

Don't allow yourself getting influenced by negativity but take actions steps that will lead to positive feedback.

Do everything you can to stay in a positive mood and SHARE YOUR PASSION, passionately.

Be real, not virtual!

Don't send old school friends half-hearted messages on Facebook, "Hey you... remember me... Guess what, I am an author now and my book needs some reviews... Want to read it?..."

Instead, call and talk with them – on the phone!

Let people hear the excitement in your voice.

Remember, most of your friends don't want to read "a book one of their friends wrote." However, all your friends want to be "the person who read the book from the next J.K. Rowling or Stephen King."

Texting and/or Facebook messaging is not ideal for conveying motivation, commitment, and excitement.

People need to hear your voice to sense that you are really "all in." So – give it to them! Share your enthusiasm!

Your goal is receiving personal, profound, and passionate reviews. Consequently, you have to be passionate when you ask for them.

*

Nothing great in the world has ever been accomplished without passion. – Georg Wilhelm Friedrich Hegel

7 THOUGHTS TO KEEP YOU GOING

"Real writers do not write because they want to be writers, they are writers because they write..."

It's never too late
to become an author.
The older you get,
the more stories
you own.

"What's a bestseller?
An author is
a success
if his book changes
one person's life."

"Struggle not
to write a bestseller
but rather a book
that matters.
Success will
follow by itself."

There are bestsellers at the end of the extra mile that still lies ahead!

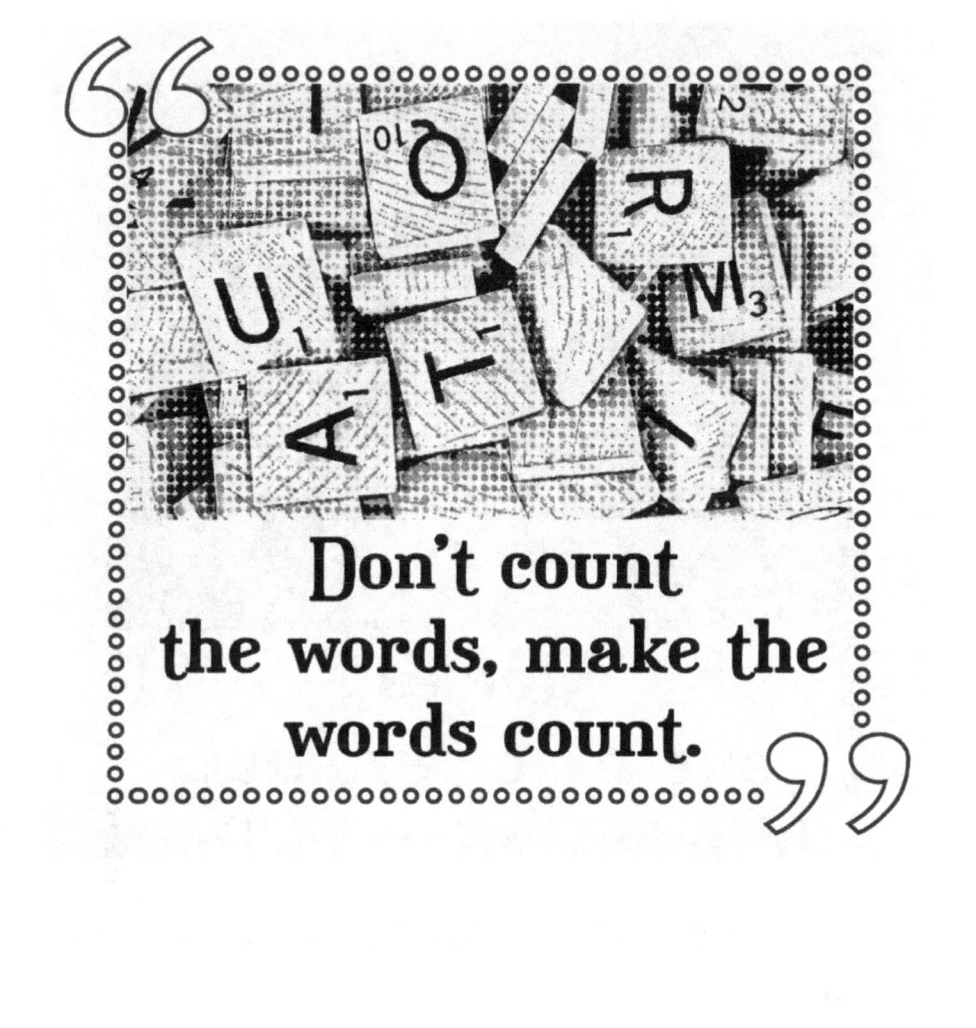

Don't count the words, make the words count.

Stories shrink or expand in proportion to the writer's courage.

Books have no limitations, except the ones you don't write.

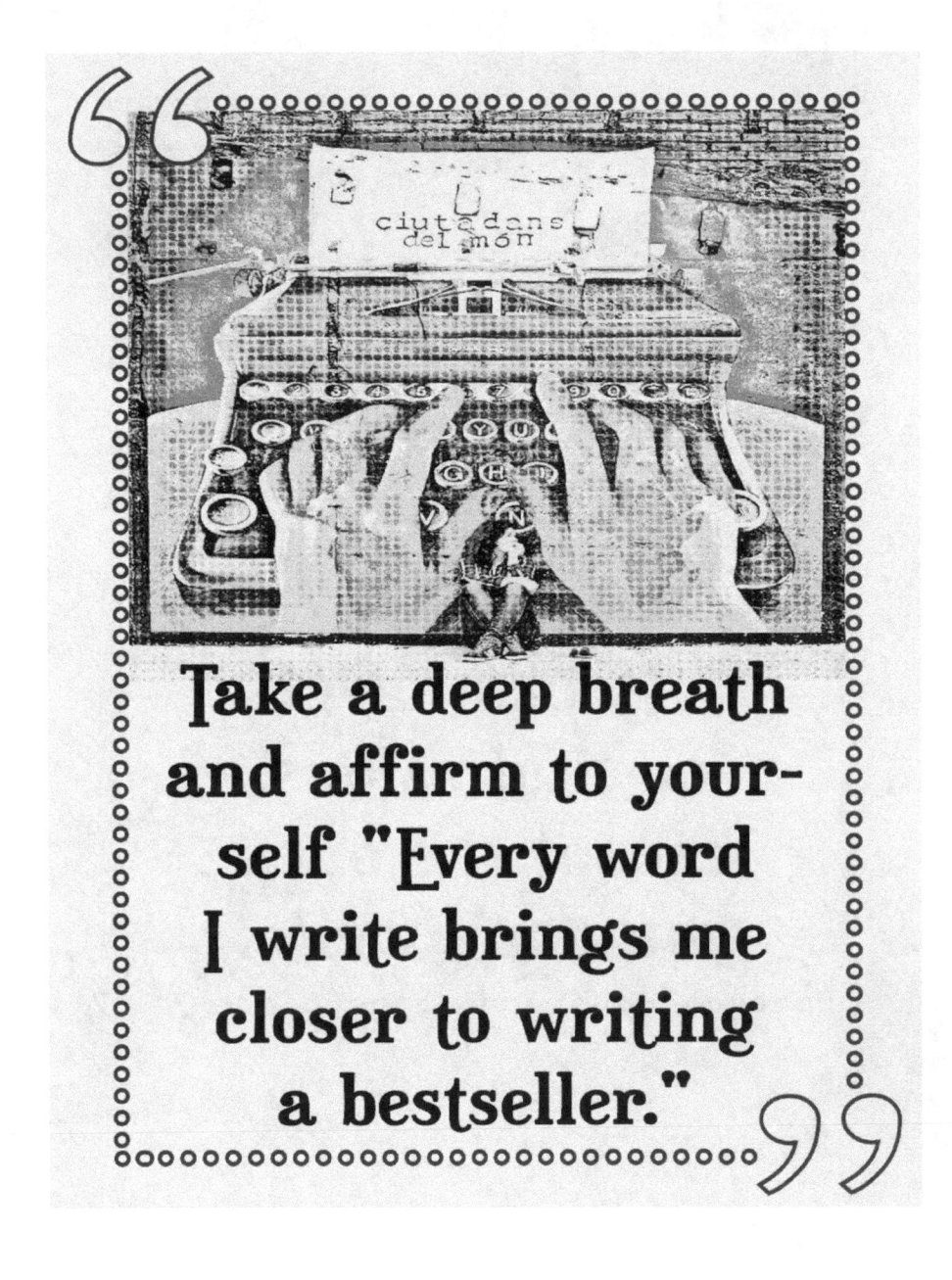

Take a deep breath and affirm to your-self "Every word I write brings me closer to writing a bestseller."

THANK YOU

for buying my book *NAKED TRUTHS About Getting Book Reviews 2018*.

If you liked it please help your fellow readers and leave a review. To succeed indie authors need to know where they can learn best practices.

Hopefully, you'll connect with me

Twitter
https://twitter.com/Naked_Determina

Facebook
https://www.facebook.com/NAKED-Truths-Words-Elaborations-Determination-1415490208749151/

Google+
https://plus.google.com/u/0/103171286110985123907

Linkedin
https://www.linkedin.com/in/gisela-hausmann-03404913/

Web:
http://www.giselahausmann.com/contact.html

Blog: *same* /free-creative-ideas.html

¿No Instagram?

* * *

To find out about other 'naked (no fluff) books' that will bring positive changes to your life as well as book deals

please subscribe at

http://www.giselahausmann.com/free-creative-ideas.html

Please know that this author respects subscribers and does not inundate them with sales emails.

* * *

Other books by Gisela Hausmann

Naked News for Indie Authors How NOT to Invest Your Marketing $$$ is a must-read for new authors. It lists the most widely used scams and how you can replace many paid-for marketing tasks by rolling up your sleeves and investing a few hours of work.

NAKED GOOD READS How to Find Readers teaches indie authors how to use the best social media platform for authors. Amazon funnels all Kindle readers to this platform, now home to 65 million readers. In 2015, I showed authors how to get book reviews from Amazon top reviewers. In this book, I explain how to find readers on Goodreads.

NAKED WORDS 2.0 The Effective 157-Word Email teaches best email practices in a 7-step system. This system is based on my work analyzing 100,000+ emails for effectiveness and personal appeal. The book helps readers in writing best marketing emails.

NAKED TEXT Email Writing Skills for Teenagers is the beginner edition of the above book.

NAKED REVIEW How to Get Book Reviews: What to do now that Amazon closed all loopholes (published in 2017) explains *What to do now that Amazon closed all loopholes*, the difference between verified reviews and non-verified reviews, and how authors can influence getting verified reviews and non-verified reviews.

The Little Blue Book for Authors Series presents essential knowledge.

About the Author

Gisela Hausmann is the winner of the
- 2016 Sparky Award "Best Subject Line" (industry award)
- 2017 IAN Book of the Year Awards Finalist
- 2016 International Book Awards Finalist
- 2016 National Indie Excellence Awards Finalist
- 2015 Kindle Book Awards Finalist
- 2014 Gold Readers' Favorite Award
- 2013 Bronze eLit Awards

Her work has been featured on Bloomberg (tech podcast) and on NBC News (biz blog), in *SUCCESS* and in *Entrepreneur*.

Born to be an adventurer, Gisela has co-piloted single-engine planes, produced movies, and worked in the industries of education, construction, and international transportation. Gisela's friends and fans know her as a woman who goes out to seek the unusual and rare adventure.

A unique mixture of wild risk-taker and careful planner, Gisela globe-trotted almost 100,000 kilometers on three continents, including to the locations of her favorite books: Doctor Zhivago's Russia, Heinrich Harrer's Tibet, and Genghis Khan's Mongolia.

Gisela Hausmann graduated with a Master's degree in Film & Mass Media from the University of Vienna. She now lives in Greenville, South Carolina.

To subscribe to Gisela's Blog pls subscribe at
http://www.giselahausmann.com/free-creative-ideas.html

Gisela's website: http://www.giselahausmann.com/
Follow her at https://twitter.com/Naked_Determina

CPSIA information can be obtained
at www.ICGtesting.com
Printed in the USA
LVHW040047240419
615328LV00036B/1024/P

9 781983 781971